ALLERGY DESENSITIZATION—ALTERING THE IMMUNE RESPONSE

Tasnim Al-Dhabbi, MD

Allergy Desensitization—Altering the Immune Response
Copyright © 2019 by Tasnim Al-Dhabbi, MD

Disclaimer from the Author:

This book is not intended for the medical attempt to treat oneself nor anyone else— and will not be held liable for any misuse of the content. This book is solely written by the Author to bring awareness to the public that Food Allergies as well as all other Allergies can be treat in the appropriate clinical setting by trained Allergists at Columbia Asthma and Allergy Clinic. Following strict medical protocols and emergency procedures. Please contact Columbia Asthma and Allergy Clinic to learn more. https://www.columbiaallergy.com/

Disclaimer from Sanjeev Jain, MD PhD:

Doctor Sanjeev Jain is not the author of this book nor did he contribute to any of the content written in this book. Dr. Sanjeev Jain did not edit the context. Tasnim Al-Dhabbi, MD is the sole author of this book. Tasnim Al-Dhabbi, MD was a Medical Student at Columbia Asthma and Allergy Clinic—she is self driven and passionate to make known to the world that food Allergies are now being treated at Columbia Asthma and Allergy Clinic.

tellwell

Tellwell Talent
www.tellwell.ca

ISBN
978-0-2288-1713-0 (Hardcover)
978-0-2288-1712-3 (Paperback)
978-0-2288-1714-7 (eBook)

Writing this book has been a great privilege.
I was a Medical Student in my last term of elective clinical rotations
in the Pacific North-West where I met Dr. Jain. Dr. Jain noticed that
I had great ambition to learn, document and teach. He promoted
my idea of writing this book and sharing the knowledge I have
learned from his experience in the past couple of decades in the
treatment of allergies. Dr. Jain saw me as a visionary. Dr. Jain gave
me a chance to partake in educating the community about his
practice. With no doubt, Dr. Jain prepared me to communicate
his teachings to the public in different community programs.

Dr. Jain helped shape my vision and gave me the confidence to
pursue myself in the field of Allergy & Immunology. The world
should know that Food Allergies are being treated! My ultimate
goal is to spread the awareness, and to provide affected families
with the basic knowledge of the treatments available in our humble
practice. My dream is to train to be an affective Allergist and train
others in hopes of expanding our practice globally—making our
treatments available to as many communities as possible. It is
time not just to diagnose Allergy, but rather treat it from its roots.
Thus, allowing affected patients to live an Allergy-Free lifestyle.
Worry-free.

•••

I wrote this book to help in making the bridge between the Scientists and the General Public—especially bringing awareness to Traditional Allergists that Allergies are now being cured. This is now an available solution to patients suffering from Allergies.

I still have a long journey before I could practice as an Allergist and do my share of change, but that should not stop me from shining a light on Dr. Jain's practice at Columbia Asthma and Allergy Clinic. Because shining a light would mean saving lives.

I pray that many more patients and practicing physicians would have the access to Dr. Jain's practice and scientific literature. I envision for the training of as many traditional Allergists as possible. I envision that kids and adults may have access to treatment in every community—worldwide.

That would be my sincerest honor.

•••

Table of Contents

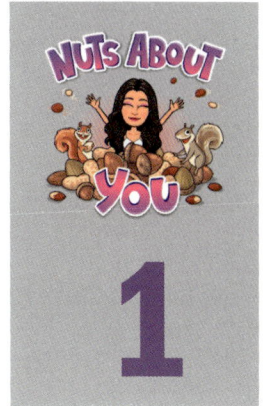

Allergies

Allergies are nothing but a systemic manifestation due to an alerted immune response. Allergies are becoming more prevalent in our global communities. Thankfully, these allergies now have a treatment. The treatment is through a process known as desensitization, which is achieved by altering the immune response and developing natural tolerance.

Allergies require proper testing in order to determine the best route of therapy.

Most patients have skin prick testing (SPT), and RAST blood testing. Other patients may have a patch test. And in the rare cases of Eosinophilic Esophagitis, an endoscopic biopsy is required.

Patients with comorbidities such as severe persistent asthma, and hyper-allergic response reactions with high levels of IgE antibodies, will require a dampening of their immune response prior to initiating desensitization in order to establish a therapeutic window.

Many patients who walk into our practice no longer want to be limited to what they can and cannot eat. And many more no longer want to be worried for their kids and remain anxious about their next accidental allergic reaction. A lot of these patients suffered a great deal. They come into our clinic knowing they can finally be treated.

Most of these patients have suffered multiple anaphylactic events that led to emergency response and resuscitation! A lot of these patients were limited to a diet whereby many of the foods people enjoy at social events and even from a snack in the pantry could be deadly! These patients are now allergy free! A great thanks goes to the proper tests and evaluation made by the hard working staff and Allergists.

Patients and their family members fly from all over the world to these clinical sites in hopes that their children can feel safe to eat a meal without the ongoing fear that accidently one ingredient can be the cause of their death!

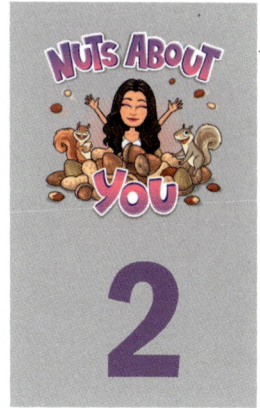

What?! Food Allergies Can be Treated?!

Yes! All food allergies can be treated. Not just in theory, but rather practically—patients with food allergies are being treated for their allergies daily. These patients like many reading this book had their allergies diagnosed, and were given an *EpiPen®* and told to avoid their noted allergens.

Some children grow out of their allergies, and others grow to have more allergies. Luckily, these allergies have a simple and a consistent way of behaving, and for which there is an equal and opposite way of altering their behavior in the patient's immune response. These allergies have learned to cause the body to react due to sensitizing the immune response by labeling the food protein molecules as foreign invaders. Allergists master the art of desensitizing these pathways by reintroducing the very same foreigner.

How? Through a process called *desensitization*. Which is basically taking an extract of the allergen and reintroducing it into the body's immune response at therapeutic levels, and slowly increasing doses until the patient develops natural tolerance.

It is through this concept that all food allergies *can* be treated and *are* being treated today.

Growing out of allergies? Some patients are just lucky enough to grow out of their allergies and developing natural tolerance over time.

Others develop more allergies to foods with similar protein complexes— on a molecular scale. Once a person develops an allergy to one food, their body is prone to developing allergies to foods of similar molecular protein makeup. This is when the immune response sees that the protein introduced is also a foreigner alongside previous foreigners. It is from this basic concept that a person can end up developing allergies to a list of foods over a period of time.

Genetic predisposition, as well as environmental factors both can play a major role in acquiring allergies.

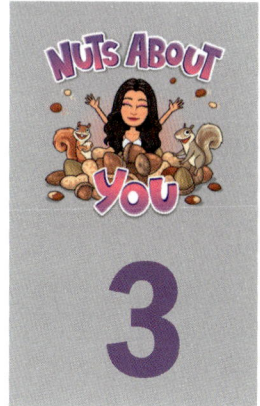

Prevalence of Food Allergies

Allergies are becoming a more and more prevalent disease in our society today. I call it the ***prevalent disease of our time***. Every community is affected by it. One classmate carries an ***EpiPen®*** for it. A child cannot attend a birthday party because of it. An adult is injecting an ***EpiPen®*** into their outer thigh muscle at your local restaurant because of it. A family member is activating emergency response because their sibling has facial swelling, wheezing and barely breathing, after taking a bite from a snack in the pantry *and* were not aware of it. The sound of a physician calling out *the time of death* as a mother cries for her child helplessly in the ICU—the loss …because of it.

•••

Please take a moment to pray for these families, for they have suffered a great deal. These are only a few stories. The world has so much more to share. These are stories I have lived to see throughout my childhood and into my adult years. Some of these children did not live to see their adult years. This is why I feel the passion to teach the world about the *root* prevention of anaphylaxis.

•••

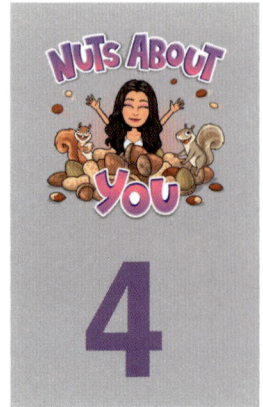

Systemic Manifestations & The Triple A's

The Triple A's in Allergy and Immunology are what is known as Asthma, Allergy and Atopy. Usually when a patient has one they have the other. Once desensitized from known allergens, patient's breathing and skin do better as they begin to build natural tolerance.

The systems to be examined and monitored for change before, during and after the treatment are:

•Skin•
•Temperature•
•Ears Nose & Throat•
•Cardiac: Heart Rate•
•Blood Pressure•
• Pulmonary: Spirometry & Pulmonary Function Testing•
•Gastrointestinal Manifestations: Bloating.
Nausea. Vomiting. Diarrhea•

These systems are to be carefully monitored for changes by the clinicians and staff as well as the patients at all times. Any changes require immediate attention.

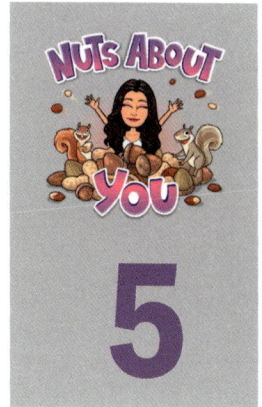

10 Fold Protection—
Sublingual Immunotherapy

Sublingual immunotherapy is the treatment of choice as a step up therapy for severe allergies and for mild food allergies with a wide list of allergens. Sublingual immunotherapy is also the treatment of choice for Eosinophillic Esophagitis and environment allergies.

The benefits seen with sublingual immunotherapy is so much more than I could explain in a few paragraphs. A few great things I would like to share with my readers are that with sublingual immunotherapy, each bottle can have up to **20 different allergens**. And patients could have multiple bottles. Some patients love sublingual immunotherapy because they could be treated for both food and environmental allergies simultaneously.

Step up therapy—the patients with anaphylactic reactions to foods generally feel comfortable starting with sublingual immunotherapy prior to going forward with oral immunotherapy.

Treatment of Eosinophillic Esophagitis— while we continue the use of swallowed inhaled corticosteroids during the course of the treatment. Some patients have proven not to require their steroids after sublingual immunotherapy is finished. Six months to a year after to the patient has reached maintenance dosing, the endoscopic biopsy is negative of eosinophils in the lining of the patient's esophagus.

Treatment of environmental allergies—some children cannot tolerate the traditional subcutaneous immunotherapy to eliminate their symptoms. These patients find it easier to start with sublingual immunotherapy and find that their allergy symptoms dissipate. Nevertheless, sublingual immunotherapy for environmental allergies has only proven to give a patient a 10-fold protection in altering their immune response. Nevertheless, *Subcutaneous immunotherapy* remains the better choice for environmental allergies.

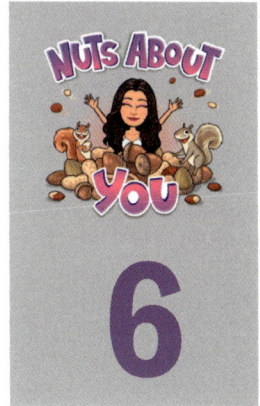

Complete Desensitization— Oral Immunotherapy

O ral immunotherapy is the current treatment of choice for the definitive desensitization to food allergies especially the foods causing anaphylactic reactions.

One would be terrified to initially think that eating one's own allergens is okay. But how? As these patients have been **ALARMED to STAY AWAY FROM their allergies!** And in anaphylactic cases, patients have been reported to use their *EpiPen®* and *activate* emergency response immediately.

This is still true in our practice and it is exactly what we teach our patients. It is **NOT** okay to be exposed to what is known to cause you an allergic reaction—especially anaphylactic reactions. Such as patients with anaphylactic reactions to peanuts, tree nuts, honey, shrimp, shell fish… etc.

However, clinically with an expert Allergist on site, when done correctly and in the right dosing, patients will eventually become allergy free. Oral immunotherapy desensitization as well as other modalities of immunotherapy in our practice, follows tight protocols. These protocols are affective in the treatment of allergy desensitization.

Oral immunotherapy requires that patients adhere to the daily consumption of their allergies at the exact amount prescribed by the Allergist. Initially the doses are in powder or liquid form diluted to an acceptable rate. Then doses are titrated and eventually patients are consuming their allergens in solid raw forms.

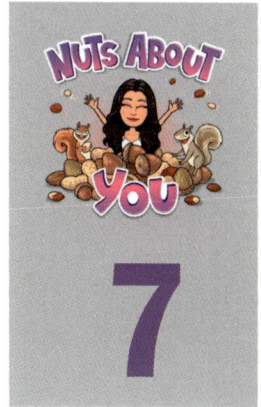

7

Achieving a Maintenance
Dose—Becoming Allergy Free

First, we build up the natural tolerance during immunotherapy in small-diluted dosages. Then once the patient passes all of their required doses and reaches a 1:1 concentration, the patient reaches a state of maintenance.

Once achieving this state, the patient is required to stay on their maintenance dose for some time before they go into a state of natural tolerance. And for which they are still required to introduce their allergens into their diet on a regular term. Sublingual immunotherapy differs to that of oral immunotherapy.

Sublingual immunotherapy; after maintenance and all oral challenges passed would require of the patient to introduce their noted allergens into their diet twice weekly to maintain natural tolerance.

Oral immunotherapy on the other hand, requires daily consumption of allergens for a year after reaching maintenance, before they would be in natural tolerance state. **After this, patients have the option to keep increasing their doses or resume with the consumption of their achieved maintenance dose.**

Interestingly, a repeated SPT would still read positive to the patient's known allergens. It would take another few years to read completely negative, although the patient has developed natural tolerance to their current dose.

It is for this reason the patients are required to continue with the intake of their maintenance dose for quite sometime, else they will lose their tolerance.

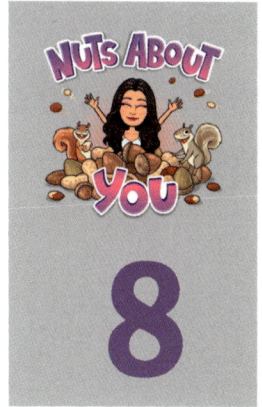

8

The Process of Elimination

The patient who comes in to our clinic with a wide range of mild to moderate food allergies tested both positive on skin prick testing and RAST blood test, would be given a list of foods to choose from.

Generally, the patient will choose *up to* twenty foods to avoid from the list and will hold from their consumption for two weeks. After the two weeks pass, the patient will choose one food at a time to consume a few times a day for four days. If the patient develops symptoms, this food would be added to their list of sublingual immunotherapy mixture in our bottle lab.

As to those foods that the patient does not develop symptoms, patient has developed natural tolerance to them and is advised to maintain consumption to the noted allergen twice weekly.

Finally, once the patient completes the first set of the process of elimination, they would choose a second set of 20 foods.

Keep in mind, that the process is the same for mild food allergies to a short range. Whereby the list is much smaller, containing a few foods to withhold from consumption for two weeks, and then introducing one at a time for the length of four days—noting the symptomatic changes.

The Allergist then writes a recipe and sends it to our bottle lab including all of the foods tested positive for allergic symptoms. After which the patient will start their sublingual immunotherapy.

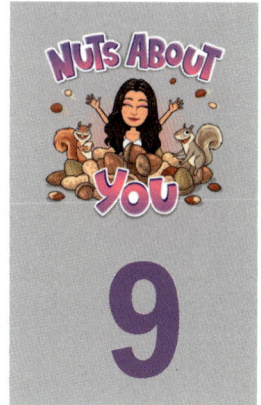

Difficult Cases of Immunotherapy

Difficult cases of immunotherapy comes in a wide spectrum. Every patient is different and requires a therapy tailored to their abilities.

Anxious patients for example, always fear a reaction during their treatments, causing doubt and constant agitation. These patients generally do well by coping mechanisms, and constant, *keen,* and thorough explanation of treatment protocol with each dose. As their level of autonomy increases, their level of comfort does the same and treatment runs smoothly. Also giving these patients the reassurance to these simple rights makes them less anxious and much more successful in their course of immunotherapy— without feeling a sense of burden.

Other difficult cases of immunotherapy are the struggle in coping with the redundancy of ingredient consumption. This is especially seen in children, as their doses become more of the raw solid form. **Some children just don't enjoy eating *peanuts* everyday** for the course of their treatment! This requires both the Allergist and the family to figure out different flavors and textures for their children to enjoy eating while simultaneously altering their immune response. Whether it is by baking their allergens into cookie dough, or mixing their dose into a small portion of fruit sauce of their choice—and once in while the ice cream milk shake. After all, we don't want to treat allergies and cause diabetes!

While in therapy, it is imperative to acknowledge the variety of choices needed for young patients and adults alike as they undergo dosage consumption and overcome their challenges.

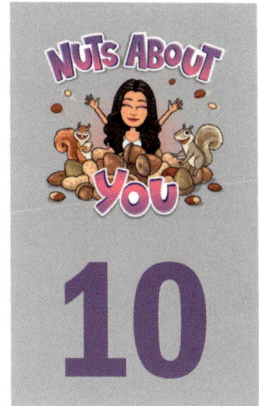

Making a Window of Opportunity by Dampening the Immune Response

I n really poor cases, some patients will require a biologic to dampen their immune response, whereby a therapeutic window is established and desensitization can be initiated safely. These patients are generally the ones with really high IgE antibody levels, severe persistent asthma and extremely poor skin conditions alongside other systemic manifestations and limited diet options.

Biologics are not for everyone. Some patients are not age appropriate, and others don't match the specific criteria.

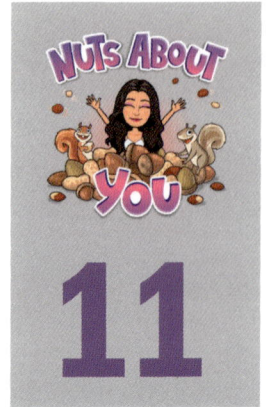

11

The Sister and Brother Nuts

S ome nuts have similar protein makeup. Desensitization to one protein mimics that of the other. In the earlier stages of desensitization, each of the similar nuts would be added to the formula. Once the doses are raw and bigger, one of the two could be eliminated as an option to our patients. And finally once desensitized to one. The other could be challenged in the later stages.

•Cashews and Pistachios • Almonds and Brazil Nuts• •Walnuts and Pecans•

These paired nuts are what we call the 'sister and brother nuts'. They share similar protein makeup. I call these the fun proteins, because they give our patients a leverage as to which nut they enjoy eating more in their required daily doses.

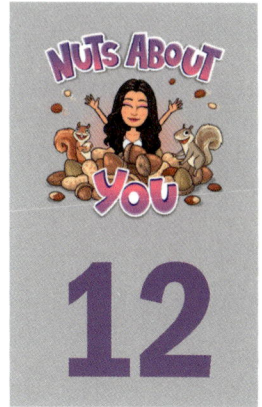

Drug Allergies

T he approach is very similar in treating drug allergies to that of food and environmental allergies.

A famous drug that sometimes requires desensitization is the antibiotic—Penicillin, famous in the treatment of the pregnant women with neuro-syphilis. This is usually seen in the hospital setting—the Allergists desensitize these patients at their bedside, through IV. Basically, the patient is treated as their becoming desensitized in small, diluted doses over a short period of time.

Another known drug allergy, which often requires treatment, is Aspirin. This drug however, is usually treated at the clinical setting. The route of treatment is usually oral, whereby we take an extract of the drug and begin desensitization until the required therapeutic dose-range is achieved for our patients.

A rare form of drug allergies that are seen and for which may have an impeccable impact on the health outcomes of our patients, is their allergies to anesthesia. These patients are the ones who are helpless if it comes a time where they may need to be operated on and require anesthesia for the length of their surgery. Generally, these patients can be desensitized in the clinical setting, but feel much more comfortable doing so in the ICU with both, the Anesthesiologist and Allergist working hand-in-hand— monitoring the patient as their doses are being administered.

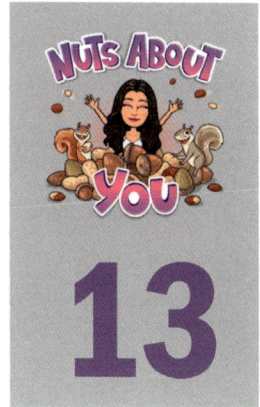

History of Allergy Desensitization

The approach to Allergy desensitization has taken its toll of tweaking. Originally, Dr. Jain and his great team of nurses and staff used to perform these procedures in the **Intensive Care Unit**.

In theory, the process of desensitization is flawless, but in practice, it needed intensive monitoring—as physical outcomes could be detrimental.

Can you IMAGINE how far things have changed from 15 years ago until this day?

Patients are *now* being desensitized at the comfort of a cozy clinical setting. They enjoy comfortably setup rooms, with the theme of their choice, come in for a few hours each session and **eat their allergies away!**

For the length of their therapy, patients do their work, homework, read, or simply use it as a leisure time to sit back and relax.

Our patients up-dose a few times in each clinical visit, and then go home on their last tolerated dose. The patients return to the clinic at the desired spaced timing—twice weekly, weekly, biweekly, and sometimes monthly. These timings are all tailored to the patient's needs and availability.

Patients who want to desensitize at a fast pace usually come in weekly and we do multiple sessions for a few hours. This process helps out patients reach their maintenance goal much faster.

Other patients space out their immunotherapy, as they cannot commit to coming in as often. They too eventually reach their maintenance goal.

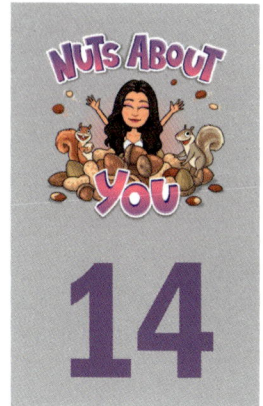

14

Environmental Allergies

Environmental allergies have two modalities of treatment and one more recent development undergoing current clinical trials. The one that is practiced by many clinical Allergists is the **subcutaneous immunotherapy (SCIT)**. In our clinic **sublingual immunotherapy (SLIT)** is the alternative route of desensitization to environmental allergies. And finally, direct **lymph node injection** is our most recent route of therapy for environmental allergies. I have provided a short outline featuring the details about this great innovation in the last chapter of this book.

Just like other allergies, the approach is the same, in the sense that an extraction of the allergen tested for causing the symptoms is administered.

SCIT remains the ***best*** option in getting rid of those seasonal and inhalant allergies as well as bee venom allergies.

SLIT on the other hand will only provide our patients with a 10-fold protection against the allergies and reduction of symptoms of asthma, allergic rhinitis, and sinusitis and skin manifestations such as atopic dermatitis. SLIT is especially used for patients with mild allergy symptoms or for pediatric patients who cannot tolerate weekly injections. **This is by far the greatest advantage for sublingual immunotherapy.**

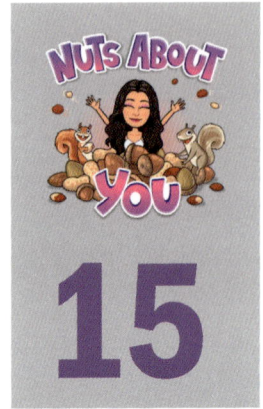

The Process of Desensitization

T he process of desensitization has different routes. Sublingual immunotherapy, oral immunotherapy and last but not least— subcutaneous immunotherapy. All these pathways to desensitization are doing one common thing; they are altering the immune response by up-regulation of the regulatory system, and down regulation of the inflammatory response. The process of desensitization requires taking an extract of the known allergen and reintroducing it into the body. This is true for all types of allergies.

Sublingual immunotherapy (SLIT) requires 24 titrated dosages to reach a maintenance dose. These doses start at a concentration of (1:3125). For severe allergies concentrations can start as low as (1:9,765,625).

Oral immunotherapy (OIT) requires 33 titrated dosages to reach a maintenance dose. These doses start at a concentration of 1:10,000). In severe allergic reactions, patients may start at much lower concentrations.

Subcutaneous immunotherapy (SCIT) requires 45 titrated dosages to reach a maintenance dose. These doses start at a concentration of (1:1,000,000). Patients with severe allergic reactions can start at a much lower dose of (1:10,000,000,000).

From each titrated concentration the patients require building up tolerance to multiple doses and amounts— **specifically measured amounts.** For example 0.05 mL of a specific recipe concentration of (1:100,000,000)… then 0.10 mL of the same concentration… and so on and so forth. Once the patient reaches a tolerated dose, they move up the scale—in the amount administered followed by the amount in concentration of their specific recipe.

The process is flawless, redundant, and extremely detailed to suit each individual patient to his or her distinctive recipe.

> •It truly is humbling to know that the magnitude effect in the treatment of allergies is initiated from a single droplet extracted from an enormously diluted solution•

> Wow! Now this is an example of a tiny molecular change showing its effects on a greater scale.
> I love Science! DON'T You?

Side note:
Drug allergies are desensitized at much higher concentrations, and require approximately 9-14 dosage titrations. The drugs must be diluted to a concentration of (1:10) and started at minimal dosage intervals.

Some drugs are desensitized by oral immunotherapy, such as Aspirin allergy.

Penicillin and Fentanyl on the other hand, are desensitized intravenously. In this type of allergy situation, Allergists are *treating* the patient as they are being desensitized simultaneously. The purpose here is not to maintain natural tolerance, but rather treat the patient for their current medical condition.

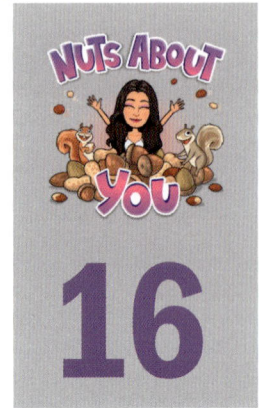

16

Altering the Body's Immune Response

Sublingual, oral and subcutaneous immunotherapies are known for **activating the stimulatory pathway by different routes, modalities and concentrations**. These therapies **activate inflammatory response** by releasing mast cells and t-helper cells amongst other inflammatory cells when recognizing an allergen.

In order for desensitization to occur, the doses must be started at a very low concentration and thus effectively introduce the allergens to the regulatory system without waking up the stimulatory response.

If stimulatory response is awakened, this is known as an allergic reaction. Patients must then be down dosed to a more diluted concentration. Failure to do so does the opposite (sensitize the patients to their allergens). Once patients tolerate their new dose, they may continue with the process of desensitization.

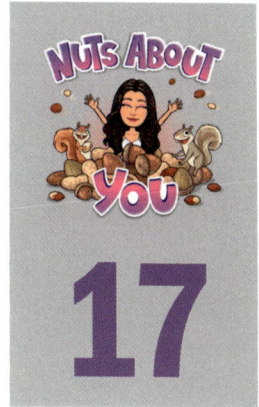

Oral Challenges

After the sublingual immunotherapy, and once the patient reaches a maintenance dose for a month, the patient returns to the clinic to begin oral challenges, whereby one food is challenged per session. If the challenge is passed, the patient is advised to introduce this food into their diet twice weekly to maintain their natural tolerance.

Oral challenges help eliminate a great deal of foods, because many foods are likely desensitized but sublingual immunotherapy.

The food challenges that fail are pushed into the next section of immunotherapy—oral immunotherapy.

So for example, if a patient has allergies to cashews, lentil, chickpea, sesame seed, banana, and a few other foods added into their sublingual immunotherapy bottle—once on maintenance dose, a patient can eliminate a few of these foods by challenging them in the clinical setting. Passing a few, if not all of them would be a great deal. Why? Because this would lessen the amount of foods consumed if oral immunotherapy is required to reach the state of natural tolerance.

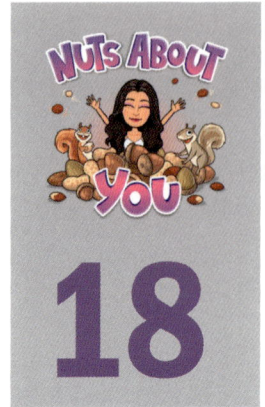

18

Risks of Immunotherapy

T he main reason to be desensitized from allergies is to get over the fear of developing a life-threatening reaction. **Anaphylaxis!** The patient and the family of the patient worry for anaphylactic reactions. This is why allergy desensitization must take place in the clinical setting, whereby the patient doses are given under careful monitoring. The allergist and nurses in the clinic are fully aware and equipped to handle such an event.

Incase of a reaction, the clinicians follow a strict protocol of handling an allergic reaction. It is very rare that our patients head to the emergency department.

Incase an anaphylactic reaction happens outside the clinical hours, patients administer their first dose *EpiPen*® **noting the time**, and head to the nearest Emergency Department. Once 15 minutes pass from the first administration of *EpiPen*®, a second dose is administered, alongside an Oral Steroid, Histamine1 and Histamine2 Blockers. An Oral Steroid and H1 and H2 Blockers are given daily for the next 3-5 days. Other supportive measures may also be initiated.

In the case of an allergic reaction, the doses for desensitization are stopped, and must be re-evaluated. Once the patient is stabilized they return to the clinic to be evaluated and start at a lower dose.

If a patient develops milder reactions, doses are revised—and some medications might be administered.

Altering the immune response requires a great deal of commitment and alertness. It is the responsibility of both the clinical staff and the patients to be keen and careful.

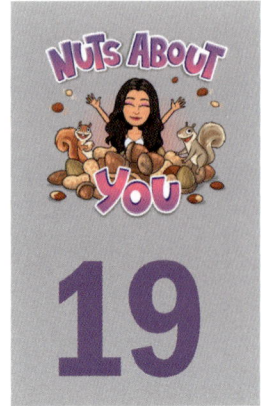

19

Benefits of Immunotherapy

I will never forget the happiness expressed by young patients after they graduated from their Tree Nut allergies, as they expressed their excitement to finally leave their nut free lunch table. They can finally join their friends not having to worry about an anaphylactic reaction.

Every time one of our patients graduate from their immunotherapy, the whole clinic celebrates their achievement because it is truly a great moment in time. It is an allergy-free milestone, which took a great deal of effort and commitment to achieve.

Being worry-free is a blissful feeling, is a mind freeing, no ingredient reading, peace of mind, and sense of relief for patients, their family and friends. It truly is a liberating sense of self to finally be able to eat the ingredient that used to be the cause of emergency response and medical resuscitation.

Allergy desensitization is such a fulfilling duty for me, and it is the greatest honour to have been passed down this knowledge from Dr. Sanjeev Jain. This has sincerely been a rewarding experience and for which I am grateful. Thank you so much!

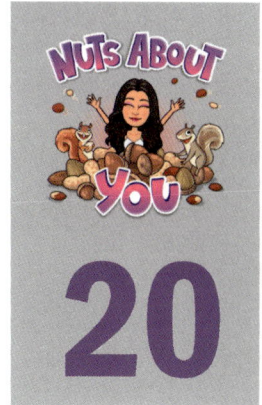

What's New in Immunotherapy?

A new innovation in treating Environmental Allergies—through lymph node injections.

Under guided ultrasonography cervical lymph node injections, Sanjeev Jain, MD, PhD and Karen Jain, MD work alongside each other as the practicing Allergist and Interventional Radiologist respectively to desensitize patients to their environmental allergies.

Why lymph node injections you may ask? Well, for starters, in order to alter the immune response it is required to introduce allergens to the **regulatory system** in order for these channels to recognize the friendly proteins not as foreigners. It is far faster to achieve a change in the immune response this way, rather than the traditional pathway of Subcutaneous Immunotherapy (SCIT).

A quick recap— SCIT is known for activating the **stimulatory pathway**. SCIT **activates inflammatory response** by releasing mast cells and t-helper cells amongst other inflammatory cells when recognizing an allergen. In order for desensitization to occur, the doses must be started at a very low concentration and thus effectively introduce the allergens to the regulatory system without waking up the stimulatory response. If stimulatory response is awakened, this is known as an allergic reaction. Patients must then be down dosed to a more diluted concentration. Failure to do so does the opposite (sensitize the patients to their allergens). Once patients do not develop a reaction, they are then clinically evaluated and are given the green light to continue with their desensitization by up dosing.

SCIT remains effective, but takes our average patient to reach maintenance dose 6 months to a year, after which patients require monthly injections for a period of 12 months to maintain natural tolerance. And it isn't unusual for patients to redevelop these allergies or acquire new ones.

The benefit of lymph node injections:

- Patients start at a much higher dose and upgrade once monthly for three months.
- Patients start at a concentration of 1:1000 on their first treatment; then 1:100 on their second treatment; and finally 1:1 on their final treatment.
- Patients with severe allergies and inflamed lymph nodes notice a change in their allergy symptoms as they dissipate.
- The clinical assessment is done by ultrasound and physical assessment showing a significant change in the size of the cervical lymph nodes. By the third session, patients' inflamed cervical lymph nodes shrink drastically in size!

— Are we treating Bee Venom Allergies through lymph node injections? **No, is the answer!**

While Environmental Allergies have a stable and predictable outcome, Bee Venom on the other hand is unpredictable in the sense that it is a toxin and as a result, patients may develop severe complications if injected to cervical lymph nodes.

The pathway to treatment of Bee Venom Allergy remains as the traditional—Subcutaneous Immunotherapy.